Adulting Life Skills for Teens

The Key to Independence
Beginner's Guide on Essential Skills
That Every Teen Needs to Learn
Now Before Leaving Home

Donna Edwin

Donna Edwin

Copyright ©2023 Donna Edwin

Table of Contents

Introduction _____ 5
   Life Skills and Their Value _____ 7

Chapter One _____ 9
   Finances or Budgeting Skills _____ 9

Chapter Two _____ 19
   Cooking or Food Skills _____ 19

Chapter Three _____ 25
   Clothing and Dress Sense Skill _____ 25
   Developing one's sense of fashion _____ 26

Chapter Four _____ 29
   Teens' Grooming Skills _____ 29
   Personal Hygiene Options For Teenagers _____ 33

Chapter Five _____ 39
   Personal Healthcare Skills _____ 39

Chapter Six _____ 45
   Social skills and Etiquette _____ 45
   Some Basic Manners That Every Teen Should Know _____ 46

Chapter Seven _____ 63
   Organizational Skills _____ 63
   7 Organizational Skills Your Teen Should Learn _____ 64

Chapter Eight _____ 71

Auto Repair and Driving Skills ___71

Chapter Nine ___77

Navigational Skills ___77

How to Teach Teens Navigational Skills ___77

Chapter Ten ___79

Coping With Emotions Skills ___79

What Makes Coping With Difficult Emotions Important? ___80

Chapter Eleven ___89

Problem-Solving Skills ___89

Chapter Twelve ___99

Time Management Skills ___99

Chapter Thirteen ___105

Decision-Making Skills ___105

Adulting Life Skills for Teens

Introduction

Once they turn 18, every child desires to leave the home and live alone. They'll be graduating, driving, and living on their own before you know it. However, maturity also brings with it unique problems and new wonders. Teenagers are not always prepared to live alone based just on their age.

There are several things your kid has to be aware of, including managing a bank account and filing taxes. It is our responsibility as educators and parents to provide teenagers with the life skills they need to succeed in the real world.

Children quickly develop into teenagers, then into adults with distinct personalities and lives of their own. To pursue a better job and carve out a place for themselves, children might need to leave the home, nevertheless. Continue reading to learn how to teach kids important life skills that can help them adjust more quickly and deal with the difficulties of life throughout this transition.

People typically believe that learning mostly takes place in classroom settings. Still, our kids pick up "adulting skills" by observing us go about our daily lives while also accompanying us, and by observing how we act in various situations.

We speculate about how they will resolve everything after they move on to live their lives. Following are thirteen fundamental life skills that young adults should be able to master by the time they leave us to live on their own.

Life Skills and Their Value

Life skills are the capacities for adaptive and constructive conduct that enable individuals to effectively deal with the demands and obstacles of everyday life.

Teenagers must acquire social and emotional skills as they develop their independence. These include interpersonal and psychosocial abilities that benefit people, such as:

- Addressing issues
- Effective communication
- Making wise decisions.
- Effective critical thinking
- Being empathetic to others
- Cultivating wholesome connections
- Self-management that is both healthy and effective

Chapter One

Finances or Budgeting Skills

While learning geography and geometry may be required for a high school diploma, some crucial life skills aren't always covered in the classroom. You can prepare yourself for financial success by using the practical skill of budgeting every day. To start building your money early, look over these 14 budgeting pieces of advice for teens.

1. Recognize Your Income

Knowing your income is the first step in creating a budget. You should add up how much money you make each month, whether it comes from a full-time job, a side hustle, or just a small allowance for helping around the house. Whatever it is, make use of it as a benchmark for your spending and saving. If the sum varies from month to month, be prudent and stick to the lower amount.

2. Produce Budget Category Lists

Create your budget categories as the next step. Two main ones should be kept in mind when creating categories: saving and spending. List all the different expenses you'll be allocating money to under these two headings. The list below includes a sample budget category.

Saving
- College fund
- Savings account
- Immediate and future purchases
- Investing for retirement
- Spending

Compulsory expenses:
- Phone bill
- Gas money
- Lunch money

Additional expenses :
- Subscription services for a gym membership
- Other meals and treats

- Fashion and accessories
- Grooming and aesthetic services
- Amusement and activities

If someone else takes care of your housing and utilities, don't include them in your budget because most teenagers don't have to worry about those things. However, if you do contribute to those, feel free to count the costs as necessary spending.

3. Select a spending plan

It's time to decide how much money to set aside for each category after you've made a list of all of them. There are several budgeting techniques you can use to accomplish this. Choose the approach that works best for you after learning more about a few different ones below.

- The "Pay Yourself First":This approach entails setting aside a certain sum of money or a certain percentage of your income as soon as possible for savings. Any money that is left over can be used however you like.

- Budgeting at zero: Want to keep track of every dollar in your spending plan? This approach is based on the notion that your net worth is zero after deducting your expenses from your income. Utilizing those estimates as a guide, calculate the cost of each budget category, then divide your income until it equals zero.

- 50/30/20 rule: This rule divides your budget into the following percentages: 50% for essential expenses, 30% for other expenses, and 20% for savings. If you don't have many expenses, you might want to put more money toward savings. These percentages can be changed to suit your needs.

4. Save first, then spend

It's a good idea to always put money into savings before you start spending once you've chosen a budgeting strategy. There is a chance that you could blow your budget one month and not have any money left over to save if you start spending before you save. You can exercise financial restraint and make it simpler to adhere to the budget you initially set by giving saving a higher priority.

5. Set goals.

Setting financial goals is a great way to spur yourself on to follow your spending plan. You might be setting money aside for a trip or your very own car. Whatever your objectives, if you stick to your spending plan and maintain good financial practices, you'll get there quickly.

6. Monitor Your Routine

Tracking your spending patterns is another useful budgeting piece of advice. To track your spending habits and think about them, use this printable habit tracker. You can determine if you can change your lifestyle realistically to save more money by keeping a record of your habits.

For instance, if you frequently splurge on iced coffee, consider a more cost-effective option like making it at home and putting it in a to-go cup. Your budget might get a significant boost from a small change to a costly habit.

7. Adjust Your Budget
Know that you can adjust your budget if you find that it isn't meeting your needs. For instance, if you frequently overspend on a necessity, like gas, change your budget to better suit those needs. If you've reduced your driving, however, feel free to put your gas money to other uses, such as savings.

Find ways to reduce your expenditure if you're overpaying on things like clothes or entertainment that are more of a wish. As an alternative, consider restructuring other non-essential expense categories to free up more money. You won't feel bad about spending money on what brings you joy once you have the availability in your budget.

8. Learn from Your Mistakes

Mistakes do occur, but what counts is what you can learn from them. Have you had to forgo a pleasant activity or settle for a less expensive option because you fell short of your financial goal? Consider why you failed to achieve your objective and how you can succeed the next time. Remember to utilize the disappointment of not reaching your goal to improve next time.

9. Boost Your Income With a Side Business

Consider starting a side business to boost your income if you discover that you'd prefer to have more budget flexibility. Teenagers can earn additional money from the convenience of their homes in a variety of ways. Consider using your skills or interests in one of these side businesses:
- Create a podcast.
- Pet-sit or stroll dogs
- Market baked goods

- Impart knowledge or instruction to others

10. Practice minimal spending

Less is more in terms of spending. Consequently, if you spend less, you'll have more money. This advice will help you adopt a minimalist way of life and mindset:

- Try a capsule wardrobe and only spend money on carefully chosen, high-quality clothing.
- Save money by going secondhand and giving old items new life.
- Look for ways to use what you already have and be appreciative of it.

11. Avoid Caving To Peer Pressure

There are numerous pressures in adolescence. You might find yourself tempted to overspend frequently, whether it's to keep up with the latest fashions or to grab a bite to eat with friends. Don't feel bad if you don't have the newest accessories or if you ask your friends to hang out in the park rather than go out to eat. True friends are always up for hanging out with you, no matter where you are or what you're wearing.

12. Ask for Help

A budgeting tip for teens is to ask for assistance when you need it. You're still learning about many facets of life, so it's acceptable to not know all the solutions. Ask your parents or other financial role models for advice if you have any. Do your research, read books written by financial professionals, or tune into podcasts online to delve deeper into more complex subjects like investing.

13. Locate an Amusing Activity

Other tools that make budgeting enjoyable and simple include technology and social media.

Chapter Two

Cooking or Food Skills

Most adults should learn how to cook because it is a necessary skill. Naturally, having a personal chef or ordering food online are benefits of being an adult. But as parents, it's crucial to pass on to our children the fundamental abilities needed to prepare a few meals for themselves to survive (and to save money).

Our teenagers will soon leave for college, so it might be beneficial to teach them a cooking technique or two so they can prepare some wholesome meals while they're away. The following list of 8 cooking skills for teens is necessary before they become adults.

1. Buying groceries

Having a fully stocked refrigerator and pantry is crucial to successful cooking. Anytime your schedules permit, take your teen along when you go grocery shopping. Take them step-by-step through the process of making a list and following it. It's beneficial to let them know that it's preferable to shop for groceries when you're not hungry. Show them the brands you typically use and the ones they ought to buy to save money.

2. How To Handle Protein

Share some knowledge or advice about the type of meat you prepare at home if your family is a meat eater. Offers advice on handling and cleaning meat as well as cleaning up any spills after handling meat. Or, if your family practices a plant-based diet, show your teen the plant-based substitutes you typically use at home. This includes dairy products like butter, cheese, and milk.

3. How to Cook Basic Meals

Certain staple dishes can be prepared quickly, easily, and healthily. Show your teen how to make these meals. Examples include soups, baked vegetables, grilled cheese, avocado on toast, omelets, scrambled eggs, and baked eggs. As an alternative, your teen's favorite social media platforms like TikTok and Instagram are loaded with recipes. You can go over these with your teenager and have them write down any ideas they have in a small notebook they can carry around. Some suggestions include three-ingredient meals and the most recent trend, three-fold tortilla wraps.

4. Smart Snack Ideas

We all recall the quantity of fast food we consumed while in college. While it's acceptable because a teen's metabolism can handle it, you must teach your teen some tasty and healthy snack hacks. Some suggestions include an apple-and-peanut butter platter, an oatmeal cookie platter, and a hummus platter with vegetables like carrots and peppers.

5. Expiration Dates of Foods
Make certain that your teen understands how to check product expiration dates. They also require information regarding the duration of storage in the refrigerator. Today, many people prepare their meals in advance, but storing food in the refrigerator for an extended period can cause it to spoil. When in doubt, dispose them.

6. Knife Skills
Allowing your teen to assist you in chopping up fruits and vegetables at home may seem very elementary. They are getting practice, so they won't dread having to do it on their own. Cutting and storing all of the vegetables for the week in advance is a useful tip. Instead of spending time cutting the vegetables, they can simply cook them all after a long day.

7. Skills in Baking

Although it's not very significant, we all go through the adult phase where we bake cookies and deliver them to friends' houses. Show your teen how to make everyday foods like banana bread, cake, and cookies. You could also learn how to make pizza dough if you want to have some freshly baked homemade pizza. It's a valuable skill to possess and also very therapeutic.

8. A Well-Balanced Diet

Understanding nutrition is just as important as knowing how to cook. This doesn't have to be lengthy, of course. The most fundamental knowledge you can impart is the importance of eating a balanced diet that includes carbs, protein, and vitamins. Simply mentioning that vegetables are your source of nutrition, bread is a source of carbohydrates, and meat is a source of protein during your meal could suffice. It's advantageous in both ways because your teen probably already knows this from school.

Chapter Three

Clothing and Dress Sense Skill

One of the more heartbreaking moments you will experience as a mother is a day you buy your child an outfit they despise. Of course, it marks a significant turning point in a child's development and is a sign that they are successfully shaping their personalities and sense of self. But it's difficult to resist having some fond memories of when they were infants.

As a mother, you won't only have to deal with this issue of clothing; you'll also have to deal with teenage cries of "But mom," and decide when to let a younger girl wear heels. But in peer interactions, job interviews, and other situations, how you are dressed can make all the difference. How can you ensure that your teenagers know what is appropriate without stifling their individuality?

Developing one's sense of fashion

It's crucial for a developing teen to feel confident in their wardrobe choices. A crucial component of developing adult confidence is feeling at ease in your clothing. Additionally, a teenager's self-esteem may depend on it. Confidence and attire are related. When people are comfortable with their style, you can tell a difference in how they carry themselves. Kids all have their ideas of what to wear that complement who they are on the inside, and clothing and identity frequently coexist.

Teenagers must understand their actions today have consequences down the road. Their future will be shaped by their teachers, parents, and potential employers. One of the major issues interviewers bring up, for instance, is how few young people in entry-level positions know how to dress for a serious job interview. They list concerns ranging from sloppy, untucked shirts to sheer blouses and peek-a-boo underwear. It matters what they think of you in a competitive job market where hiring is more difficult than ever.

Introduce the idea of appropriate attire.
Every parent is aware that lecturing their children about appropriate attire will only result in an eye roll. It's better to create an environment where your developing teen feels free to make decisions without feeling pressured by you as their parents. Give them a list of the most important things to think about as a start. Discuss with them how perception frequently matters even though it shouldn't and how you decide what to wear to different occasions. Encourage them to investigate these crucial ideas without lecturing.

- Is the clothing appropriate for the weather?
- Will they feel at ease using it and participating fully?
- Does the attire fit the "mood" of the occasion?

- Is this a casual or formal setting?

Additionally, this is a good time to bring up the notion that fashion benefits them, not the other way around. Each person can choose from a variety of outfits and skirt designs. Pantsuits can pass muster as cocktail attire. Men in the modern era can play with color. It's not necessary to permanently lose one's sense of style to dress with awareness. Simply put, it refers to a person becoming old enough to comprehend how they present themselves to others and how to take advantage of that as they mature.

Chapter Four

Teens' Grooming Skills

For youth to preserve their health, they must understand the significance of excellent personal cleanliness. Keeping one's body clean, promoting good health, and preventing disease are all goals of personal hygiene .Until late in childhood, kids pay attention to basic personal hygiene practices like covering their mouths when they cough and washing their hands after meals.

The number of new habits that are essential to a teen's health and well-being, however, expands as they approach puberty. Parental guidance can help your teen establish healthy personal hygiene practices. The significance of teenagers maintaining good personal hygiene is covered in this chapter, along with tips on how to achieve it and the role that parents can play.

Similar to how it is for children and adults, maintaining excellent hygiene is crucial for a teen's health. Teenagers' special motivations for maintaining personal hygiene go beyond the generic ones.

It promotes sanitation and protects against disease and infection exposure. Teenage ladies can avoid dangerous infections, for instance, by keeping themselves clean throughout their period.

They can remain at ease around people thanks to it. This might increase a teen's self-esteem and confidence while also inspiring them to live a healthy lifestyle. It also aids in their adjustment to the social mores of adulthood, when maintaining one's hygiene is a sign of one's character.

Personal hygiene is crucial because children experience new changes during puberty, including the development of body hair and an increase in body odor. They benefit from good hygiene to keep their privates fresh and to prevent body odor.

They may be able to maintain discipline and concentration on their objectives with its assistance.

Why Is Personal Hygiene Vital During Teens?

Similar to how it is for children and adults, maintaining good hygiene is crucial for a teen's health. Teenagers' specific motivations for maintaining personal hygiene go beyond the general ones.

It promotes cleanliness and protects against disease and infection exposure. Teenage girls can avoid potential infections, for instance, by keeping themselves clean during their period.

They can remain at ease around people thanks to it. This might increase a teen's self-esteem and confidence while also inspiring them to live a healthy lifestyle. It also aids in their adjustment to the social mores of adulthood, where maintaining one's hygiene is a sign of one's character.

Personal hygiene is crucial because children experience new changes during adolescence, including the development of body hair and an increase in body odor. They benefit from good hygiene to keep their privates fresh and to prevent body odor.

They may be able to maintain discipline and concentration on their objectives with its assistance.

Personal Hygiene Options For Teenagers

Personal hygiene is a broad term that includes many different types of self-hygiene routines, including bathing, hand washing, tooth brushing, etc. Here are the different types of good hygiene practices.

1.Skincare

Teenagers' skin may become more oily as they enter puberty. An environment for the growth of germs is created by oily skin, which collects dust and dirt. Numerous skin conditions, including blackheads and acne, are brought on by it. As a result, it is beneficial for a teen to establish a good skincare routine that includes regularly washing their face with water and mild soap. If the teen has ongoing skin problems, consult a dermatologist. Skincare products like gentle cleansers and creams for acne can be prescribed by the doctor.

2. Haircare

Teenagers are more social than young children. As a result, their skin and hair frequently become soiled. Hormonal changes may also cause the hair to become oily and odorous. The issue is only made worse by the hair's thickness. Encourage your teen to wash their hair with mild shampoo twice or three times per week as a result. Following consultation with a trichologist, they may also nourish their hair by using some homemade or alternative hair care products.

3. Nail care

Teenagers enjoy letting their nails grow out, giving them various shapes, and designing them. However, fingernails are the perfect environment for bacteria to grow. When using the hands to eat, these bacteria can enter the mouth. By touching the face, germs may also spread to the skin or enter the mouth, eyes, and nose. Therefore, your teen needs to keep up with nail hygiene. A nail brush can be used to remove the dirt. Additionally, weekly nail trimming should help remove dirt and lessen the likelihood of painful ingrown nails.

4. Oral care

Poor oral hygiene can result in issues like bad breath and tooth decay. Make sure your child flosses and brushes their teeth twice daily. Additionally, they ought to rinse their mouth with either water or mouthwash after meals.

5. Washing hands

Washing hands is important because they can carry germs to almost any part of the body. Before and after eating, playing outside, caring for or playing with pets, using the bathroom, and any other time they come into contact with a contaminated surface call for washing hands.

6. Bathing

Body odor appears as a result of the emergence of a new type of sweat gland in the genital and armpit regions during adolescence. Body odor is caused by bacteria on the skin that feed on the substances in the compounds in the sweat from these areas. Because of this, you must explain to your teenager that bathing, especially after exercise, aids in removing sweat and bacteria and reduces body odor. To reduce sweating, they might also use an antiperspirant.

7. Toilet hygiene
Although it's probably not a brand-new hygiene habit for teenagers, it needs to be updated once they enter puberty. Teenagers typically have some secretions from their genitalia, so they should be advised to wipe them every time after using the restroom and wash them while taking a bath.

8. Menstrual hygiene
When teaching menstrual hygiene to a teenage girl, it is important to emphasize tracking periods, using sanitary products like tampons or sanitary pads (either reusable or disposable), and properly discarding these items after use. A teenage girl should also be given instructions on how to use

these products properly and how often to replace them.

9. Shaving

Depending on how their hair grows, teenage boys may develop a mustache or beard. You can get shaving cream and a razor designed for teenagers for the boy if he wants to shave. Show them safe ways to trim their facial hair without hurting themselves. Similarly to this, teenage girls who wish to have their underarm hair removed should be advised of the necessity of using sterile instruments, to use caution when shaving their genital area, and to avoid doing so unless necessary. Additionally, instruct them on proper after-shave skin care and the reasons they should not share their accessories with others.

10. Clean clothing and footwear

It's critical to switch out your clothes daily, especially your socks and underwear. Sweat and other bodily fluids that can harbor germs are retained by clothing. Teenagers who dress and walk in clean shoes and clothes can successfully fight puberty-related problems like body odor and stinky feet.

Chapter Five

Personal Healthcare Skills

The majority of your child's medical decisions, if not all of them, have been made by you. However, if you have preteens or teenagers, now is the time to start including them in healthcare decisions and giving them more freedom to manage their care.

Why Incorporate Teens?
The age of the majority is rapidly approaching. Therefore, it is now necessary to assist teenagers in becoming more self-reliant, and part of that includes maintaining their health.

This can be as easy as having them call in a prescription to be picked up or as difficult as letting them choose a new healthcare practitioner. This teaches teenagers how to prepare ahead of time, make decisions, and take responsibility for their actions. They'll require these abilities when they're adults.

Kids' Involvement

As any parent of a preteen or teen knows, giving children additional tasks don't guarantee that they'll carry them out. You still have a responsibility to support, reaffirm, reinforce, and monitor the obligations you assign to your child.

As children get older, it's especially crucial for those who have chronic illnesses—like diabetes or asthma—to become independent when it comes to medical treatment and to understand everything they can about their problems.

Children with special needs and developmental impairments can also learn to handle a variety of caregiving tasks. When deciding how and when to start preparing your child for more independence, it is frequently helpful to wait until a doctor, social worker, or another medical professional gives the go-ahead.

Regulations by Age
about around age 12:

Use age-appropriate terminology to explain any medical conditions to your children. Have them then say it back to you. This aids children in learning about their conditions.Encourage young patients to meet with doctors alone (without you in the room). Children can speak openly and express questions that they might be ashamed to ask in your presence thanks to the trust that is built up between patient and clinician.

Ask your children to learn why and what medications they take. It's important to mention now whether a child has ever experienced an allergic reaction to a medication, such as penicillin.Children with chronic conditions should be aware of who to contact for any potential medical equipment or supplies.

Within the age of 14, teens should:
- Know if you they have ever undergone surgery, had an operation, or undergone any severe medical procedures.

- Know your family's medical history, including whether diabetes or heart disease runs in the family. Has cancer claimed a life?

- Have the names and phone numbers of every doctor you've ever had.

- Understand how to refill a prescription and fill one.

- Maintain a list of all medications they are taking, along with dose instructions.

Teenagers around the age of 17 should :

- Examine your options for a primary care physician for adults. Kids frequently decide to go to the family physician that their parents do.

- Possess copies of medical records or know where to get them (for instance, from a doctor's office or school).

- Become familiar with their health insurance details and how to contact a representative.

- Understand how to obtain specialist referrals, if necessary.

Upon reaching maturity, individuals are aware of the restrictions on health insurance coverage. When dependent children's parental insurance coverage expires, make arrangements for independent medical care.
Meet with the local Social Security office to apply for benefits if necessary.

Chapter Six

Social skills and Etiquette

The majority of parents think of teaching manners as telling a preschooler to say "please" and "thank you," but excellent manners go well beyond those words, so it's crucial to continue teaching your child good manners into the teenage years.

Unfortunately, many teenagers aren't learning fundamental social skills in the digital age, like proper cellphone usage. And despite having learned numerous manners in the past, teens frequently forget them. Teenagers occasionally go through phases where they lose all regard for manners to look cool. Other times, they behave a little carelessly and forget to be courteous.

The future of a nice, considerate, and well-mannered teen can be greatly benefited by raising them. Teens who act appropriately will be treated with greater respect, which may benefit them socially and academically.

Some Basic Manners That Every Teen Should Know

Teenagers occasionally require some basic etiquette refresher training. When they spend time with their friends, they are more likely to acquire some undesirable habits or occasionally become lethargic.

You should make sure your teen consistently practices the following manners:
- When they've done something wrong they should apologize.
- Obtain consent before acting.
- When they're having a face-to-face chat, they shouldn't take calls. They should also refrain from grabbing things out of other people's hands.
- When speaking, make eye contact.

- When speaking to individuals in person, avoid texting and using social media.
- When they need to interrupt or if they unintentionally run into someone, they should say "excuse me."
- Learn the art of saying "please" and "thank you."
- When greeting a new person, shake hands.
- Maintain good personal hygiene by sneezing into their elbow and coughing into their elbow.
- Answer questions when they are asked and use proper terminology.
- When dining, exercise good table manners.
- Wait for your chance to speak in a conversation.
- People who give them things should receive thank-you cards.

Teenagers might easily forget about common courtesy in today's digital age. However, it's impolite to grunt in response to a question from Grandma or to text while eating. Therefore, it's crucial to instruct your kid on courteous and kind ways of speaking, interacting with others, and responding to them.

The importance of good table manners and ways to promote good manners

You may train your teen to behave properly in the same way that you train them to do anything else:

- Make your expectations clear.
- If necessary, impose consequences on your adolescent.
- Discuss the advantages of using excellent manners.
- When your kid makes a mistake, try not to lecture them or make them look bad in front of others. Instead, when you notice an issue, have a private discussion about their manners.

The one thing that is not typical is disrespect. Take immediate action if your teen is being disrespectful to you. Make it plain that you won't accept being treated unfairly. Take away your teen's privileges and let them earn them back through courteous behavior.

Provide your teen with chances to exercise good manners. Opportunities for kids to hone their abilities include asking the wait staff for an additional drink in a restaurant or returning an item to the store.

You can also discuss fictional people from television or movies and their interactions with others. What impact do manners have on people's lives? Play a role when your teen is getting ready to enter a new circumstance. For instance, discuss how to greet their parents with them before they choose a prom date. Alternately, role-play how to check in at the desk before they leave on their own for an appointment.

Mention exemplary manners to your teen when you observe them. Your input can be a crucial part of your teen's capacity to pick up new manners and hone his skills. If you tell them when they're doing a good job, they'll be more inclined to keep up the excellent work.

Social Skills for Teens

As adults, we frequently act without a second thought because our social skills have become so ingrained in our daily lives.Our social skills have been so honed over the years that they almost come effortlessly, whether we're meeting new people, talking with the clerk at the grocery store, or showing sympathy for a sick friend.

However, compared to us, our teens haven't had nearly the same experiences.

Without any fault of their own, it's possible that they haven't had the same opportunities to hone those skills as we did when we were kids.In contrast to us, our children are spending more time than ever in front of a screen, which experts say is negatively affecting their social skills.

Our children have much too much access to social media sites like Instagram, Snapchat, and TikTok where they may connect and communicate via texting rather than face-to-face communication.

However, not only may our children benefit from learning a few crucial social and communication skills now, but their future success in life also heavily depends on how well they use those abilities once they enter adulthood. Their social skills and capacity to communicate with others will have an impact on everything, including their career and potential romantic relationships.

The ability to interact with others is something that must be taught to our children. Don't send your child into the world without teaching them these crucial social skills that your teen needs to learn right away.

Ten Vital Social Skills You Must Teach Your Teen Right Away

1. How to make eye contact

Teenagers are renowned for avoiding eye contact, even though it is unquestionably one of the most crucial social skills. Some teenagers avoid staring people in the eye for a variety of reasons, including phone distractions, shyness, disinterest, low self-esteem, or perhaps they're not in the best mood. However, a gentle reminder is frequently necessary since they simply aren't aware of what they're doing (or, in this case, not doing).

All teenagers struggle with eye contact, despite it being one of the more crucial social skills you should teach your adolescent. Here are a few pointers to assist your teen get the hang of appropriate eye contact if they find it difficult or even anxiety-inducing.

Adhere to the 50/70 rule. Try to maintain eye contact 50% of the time while speaking and 70%

of the time while listening. This is only a general rule of thumb; don't get too mathematical with it.

Attempting to maintain eye contact for between five and ten seconds at a time is another tactic. Then take a few seconds to casually glance to the side before making eye contact again. Make sure to glance away gently whenever you turn your head. You could come out as apprehensive or shy if you look away too rapidly (with your eyes darting).

2. Addressing People by Name
Wassup, buddy! may have been our kids' go-to greeting for friends (and probably others) during the past few years.
"Hi, girlfriend! How's it going, bruh?
But as they become older, they need to improve their social skills. They must learn the correct way to address people by name and use those names when making introductions, whether they are speaking with a teacher, college professor, or the parents of a friend.

The strongest link to an individual's uniqueness is their name. It not only makes the other person feel special, but it also leaves a positive impression when our kids make a point of remembering someone's name before calling them by name.

3. Mutual Communication Skills

It could take some repetition to help our children master the skill of communicating. To keep things simple, kids can start by honing a few fundamental question-and-answer techniques. Kicking back questions after questions are one of the fundamental communication norms. In other words, our children ought to reply, "I'm wonderful, how about you? ", when asked, "How are you today? Another illustration would be if someone asked, "Do you have any significant plans for the summer break? Yes, we're going to the beach, how about you?"

The usual rule of thumb is to show others the same amount of interest that you display in them, even though this may not always be the case (overdoing it may make things a little odd). (Even better is if our children initially exhibit interest in others!)

4. Getting Along with Adults

Our kids might not have had a lot of experience conversing with adults, other than parents, family, and the rare one-on-one instructor engagement. As a result, it's only natural for their insecurity to come through when they have a conversation with their friend's parents, a college professor, or their new boss at work.

Perfectionism is a process that requires practice. Sure, as they develop the confidence they could stumble and stammer a little, but the more adult relationships we encourage our children to make, the more they'll start to hone in on their communication abilities. With time and effort, they'll overcome their fear and anxiety while conversing with adults, close the generational gap, and develop more mature social skills.

5. Body Language Analysis (to Avoid Awkward Situations)

Body language and facial expressions, which we don't often explicitly communicate, can reveal a lot about our own and others' thoughts and emotions. Not only do our children need to learn how to interpret body language in others, but they also need to be aware of the fact that their nonverbal communication is doing most of the talking. In fact, according to some research, up to 60% of what a person expresses verbally is expressed non-verbally.

Our kids can gain a lot from learning a few nonverbal communication signs, from folded arms, which suggest being "locked off" and protective, to facial expressions that can transmit a variety of emotions.

6. The Right Introductions

Teenagers are known for striking up informal conversations with strangers. And, for the most part, that's okay in the friend world ("Umm, huh...

so, this is Julie. We have class together. However, as they grow older, our children will need to have a few fundamental "correct introduction" abilities under their belts.

Many people believe introducing themselves or others is so difficult that they skip it entirely. But it's fairly easy. Everything comes down to speaking to the person you want to honor first. For instance, if you want to introduce your college roommate to your grandmother, turn to your grandmother and say, "Grandma, I'd like you to meet my roommate, Peter Robison," before turning to Peter and saying, "This is my grandma, Mrs. Lawson."

As a general guideline, you should always introduce yourself properly when you're among adults, such as your parents, grandparents, siblings, teachers, coworkers, bosses, etc. (Hint: Don't forget to make eye contact when doing so.)

7. The Capacity to Listen

If we're being completely honest, most teenagers don't listen well. Indeed, the majority of them have poor listening skills. However, they are not truly to blame. They probably didn't learn how to listen to anyone. What they've discovered by imitating others is that listening essentially entails putting on a show for as long as necessary so they can rejoin the conversation (or jump back on their phone).

However, listening—really listening—is a talent that requires practice to acquire. Our children must put their phones away (which is a trick in and of itself), listen to understand rather than respond to what is being said, and keep their opinions to themselves to be good listeners (unless asked, of course). Knowing what not to say when it's your turn to speak is another component of listening well.

8. How to Be Compassionate

The majority of teenagers are completely preoccupied with their own lives. It's entirely normal, which is fantastic news. Since they are undergoing such significant change, they need to keep their attention on themselves as they grow apart from us and establish their own identities. The bad news is that teens who don't seem to care about anything can be frustrating to talk to, which is precisely why they should learn how to show empathy and sympathy for others.

Many teenagers find it difficult to do this on their own. They must be led and taught to enquire about other people's lives and to show empathy and sympathy when others discuss the difficulties in their own life. Additionally, they can learn by observing and listening to us. They will be more likely to act similarly in their own lives if they hear and see us demonstrating concern, care, and compassion for others as well as a sincere willingness to step in and assist.

9. How to Leave an Outstanding First Impression

Do you know that it takes the average person three seconds to form an opinion about one of our teenagers after meeting them? In a split second, someone will judge our teen's appearance overall, body language, mannerisms, demeanor, and how they are dressed. It's also quite difficult to change a negative impression after it's been formed. First impressions might not be important when they're hanging out with friends, but they will be important when they land their first job, go off to college, and begin their careers.

Our kids can start by smiling, dressing appropriately (sorry, hoodies and flip flops won't cut it in a job interview), being courteous, attentive, polite, and on time, regardless of whether they want to make a great impression on a date with a boy or girl they're crushing on, when they go on a date with that person. Making a great first impression also requires being genuine rather than acting phony.

10. How to Communicate Clearly

Because they are obsessed with mobile devices and social media, it is well recognized that today's youth don't exercise their "socialization muscles" nearly as much as those in previous generations. Sadly, our children are not learning the essential communication skills they require to thrive. Some teenagers struggle with even seemingly basic abilities like making small chats, handling conflict, engaging in reciprocal conversation, and developing the knack of avoiding prolonged, uncomfortable awkward pauses.

We owe it to our children to teach them how to sarly both offline and online. We'll be arming them with the ability to think quickly, pick up on verbal and nonverbal cues, and learn how to truly connect with others without stress, anxiety, or awkwardness by giving them plenty of opportunities to put their face-to-face communication skills to the test, even if they fight us a little.

Chapter Seven

Organizational Skills

The reason why Organizational Skills Are Important

We want our teens to show that they have strong organizational abilities for a variety of reasons. Research demonstrates that organization is advantageous in a wide range of development areas. We observe higher levels of stress and distraction when things are disorganized. Lack of organizational skills causes students to face more academic difficulties, receive lower grades, and interact poorly with teachers. The explicit teaching of organizational skills through targeted interventions is necessary for many adolescents and young adults with special learning needs. Even small gains in organizational abilities can reduce signs of inattention and boost academic performance.

7 Organizational Skills Your Teen Should Learn

1. Differentiate between being neat and messy

If the child can distinguish between a tidy, organized space and a cluttered one, that is one of the first things we check when we start working on organization skills. Despite how straightforward it may seem, some people with particular learning needs may not assess their surroundings in the same manner as you do.

Ask your child to identify areas that appear neat and organized by first bringing up some online images. Photos of unusually messy rooms, cluttered spaces that are organized, and spaces that may benefit from some tidying-up should all be displayed. Then proceed to your home, where you may even need to create some of your messes.

Can your kid recognize and distinguish the differences? If not, it's unlikely that you will be able to agree on what being organized entails until you are. Continue your efforts to develop applicable definitions of an organization that you and your teen can both understand.

2. Making Use of Designated Locations

A place for everything, and everything in its place.Establish a special location for important items with your teen. Determine where each item belongs by starting with one category, such as "school supplies" or "morning routine." Use a label maker to indicate the designated place for things if your teen benefits from visual cues. Create an album on your teen's phone or tablet and have them take pictures of how a space appears after everything is put away. The photo album will help them put everything back where it belongs when they need to find something or when they are finished with it.

3. Starting With a Clean Environment

Our brains function better in tidy, uncluttered spaces. Teach your teen to prepare their workspace before each work session by spending a few minutes doing so. Place distractions away and keep the necessary learning materials nearby. Incorporate your teen's preferences for furniture, décor, and location when creating a tidy, organized workspace if they don't already have one in your home. The more enjoyable they find the environment, the more devoted they will be to keeping it clean and orderly.

4. Prepare The Night Before

Checklists and daily agendas are essential tools to use to stay organized and on schedule, especially as the day comes to a close. Even though we may wish for our teen to "just know" how to plan independently for the following day's activities, using an end-of-the-day reminder list may be a more practical approach.

Teach your teenager to prepare all the supplies and equipment they'll need the following day the night before. They'll be more likely to use time management and self-management abilities to carry out the plan they've created, in addition to developing the habit of organization.

5. Using A Weekly Organization Checklist

It's best to organize in small "tidy up" sessions rather than all at once, which can quickly turn into a monumental task. To prevent a significant accumulation of tasks, teach your adolescent and young adult to complete a few different organizational tasks each day.

Together, start by outlining all the cleaning and organizing tasks for the upcoming week. If a task needs to be done every day rather than just once a week, mark it with an asterisk (*). Once that is done, distribute the tasks equally among the seven days of the week. Give your child the freedom to choose which chores and when to complete them. As soon as your child completes the tasks on the checklist, reward them. Place the checklist in a visible place.

6. The Ohio Law

You might teach your adolescent how to prioritize their tasks in addition to teaching them how to use a weekly organization checklist. The OHIO Rule, also known as "Only Handle It Once," has been promoted for years by process engineers and organization specialists for particular tasks like email, paperwork, and homework.

Giving your teen the ability to initiate and finish tasks as soon as they are presented with them—instead of putting them on hold or returning to the same tasks repeatedly—will empower them to succeed.

7. How to Identify Overwhelm and Overload

Even with the use of many of the aforementioned techniques, your teen will occasionally struggle with organization. Everybody experiences it. It's more crucial to teach your teen how to identify when their organizational methods have failed when they've strayed from using the success-promoting tools, and when they're overburdened.

Overwhelming and overload are the times for many teenagers and young adults with special learning needs to turn to problem behaviors rather than asking for assistance. You can all avoid a lot of stress by teaching your teen to spot these warning signs and what to do at the moment to pause and reset the organization system.

You Should Act In The Ways You Want To Be Seen

Modeling the behaviors you want to see in your teen or young adult is crucial if you want them to adopt these new habits. It's hardly fair to hold your child to a higher standard if they witness you fumbling around in the morning for your keys or arriving at appointments without the necessary supplies. Make sure your own are in order before attempting to improve their planning, organization, and time management.

Chapter Eight

Auto Repair and Driving Skills

Teenagers enjoy learning how to drive because it allows them to travel at will, hang out with their friends, and become more self-reliant. They must learn how to handle any problems or circumstances that may arise, as much as they might enjoy their newfound freedom. Parents must impart the fundamentals of car maintenance to their children to properly prepare them. The following is what parents can do to encourage their teenagers to drive more responsibly.

1. Examining the engine's oil
Our cars cannot function without engine oil. With the impact of nanotechnology on the automotive industry, it is especially crucial to maintain oil at the proper levels for the long life of modern engines. Teach your child when to change the oil; this is of utmost importance. Another topic you

should discuss with them is the type of oil their car uses. Tell them to check the oil and make sure it's full, and emphasize that the oil should be black or brown. They must be aware that they should take their vehicle to the mechanic to have them take a look if there are any odd objects in the oil.

2. How to change a tire

Your teen must be ready to deal with a flat tire. They must be prepared for it because it can occur anywhere, at any time, and they must know what to do in such a demanding but typical circumstance. Assure them that they understand how to use safety precautions, such as parking in a secure area of the road and using safety reflectors. They should be knowledgeable about the equipment needed to change the tire, including how to locate the spare tire and successfully mount it. First, they must remove the old tire by using a car jack. The performance of the car is significantly influenced by the tire quality as well. Make sure your teen has confidence behind the wheel by fitting the car with high-quality tires like Toyo tires.

3. Replenishing the windshield fluid

For dealing with various weather conditions, you must have enough brand-new windshield fluid. Even though it's one of the simpler car maintenance chores they must complete, your teen needs to know how to refill the windshield washer fluid. Make sure they use the appropriate windshield fluids depending on the weather they're driving in because having a cloudy windshield can lead to a lot of issues. They will require bug spray in the summer, and when the weather turns chilly, they should use a de-icer. To be on the safe side, they can choose an all-in-one product for the year.

4. Convertible car seat installation and upkeep

Approximately 75% of parents install convertible car seats incorrectly. This is because various manufacturers have various standards and recommendations for installing their particular brand of the car seat. Before involving your teen, you should learn how to do it properly yourself because it's one of the most crucial things for the safety of your infant or toddler.

The best convertible car seats currently on the market should be found first by conducting in-depth research and reading expert online reviews. After purchasing the model that best suits your requirements, is sure to read the owner's manual for your car as well as the instruction manual. You should be able to get all the information you need from these on how to install your seats properly and safely as well as where to do it.

5. Tire inflation
Driving safely depends on having properly inflated tires. Underinflated tires can be very problematic for you and decrease the overall life of the tires. That means ensuring the tires are inflated and checking the tire pressure just once a month can extend the life of the tires and help you avoid hazardous situations. Teach them how to

use a digital tire gauge to check the air pressure in their tires and make sure they understand that they should do it when the tires are cold because they warm up while they are driving. Tell them to compare the results with the amounts specified as recommended by the manufacturer using the information they obtained from measuring the pressure. They can use the digital gauge's readings as a guide to determine when it's time to fill their tires with air.

6. Cleaning the car

Washing the car at home is one of the simpler aspects of car maintenance, so it shouldn't be too difficult for your teenagers to handle. They should park their car in the shade and begin washing it when the engine is cool. The car needs to be thoroughly washed down with cool water first. First, they should try to wash everything away with water. Then comes the scrubbing process, which requires using a sponge and beginning at the top of the car. Use of car wash detergent is advised because it is kinder to the finish of the car. Inform them that they should dry the car with towels to avoid water spots. To put the finishing touches on the project, they can use tire lubricant to make the tires shiny.

When they first start driving, you should teach your child some fundamental car maintenance techniques. To ensure that your teen drives responsibly while enjoying their newfound freedom after receiving their driver's license, go over all the essentials of driving a car.

Chapter Nine

Navigational Skills

In the last month of a year-long program to teach kids life skills, navigation is the focus! It will be an exciting voyage as we educate teens on navigational skills, including educating them about maps, transportation, and more.

How to Teach Teens Navigational Skills

First Week: Navigation Tools

The many categories of navigational aids should be discussed with your teen. GPS systems, mobile apps, MapQuest, and even paper maps are all options!

Learn how to read a map and use a compass with your teen. If technology fails, these will be useful.

Second Week: Ways of Getting Around

Talk about the various forms of transportation and how to use them. Buying train or bus tickets, purchasing airline tickets, taking the subway, or even renting a car. In particular, if they will be going back and forth for college, discuss comparing the costs of the various possibilities.

Third Week: Safe Neutral Negligence

Make sure your kid understands how crucial it is to be cautious of their surroundings, especially in strange places. observing the business signs you pass, noting the street names, and keeping an eye on the gas gauge.

Fourth week: Negotiating

Put the various tools to use in everyday life, even if it's just for a short journey to the grocery store or the kids' school.

If you can, take a trip in a different kind of vehicle together.

Chapter Ten

Coping With Emotions Skills

Many people believe that only grownups may experience stress and other tough emotions. While this may have been true once upon a time, today's teenagers have a lot on their plates. Many people think that teenage period is a carefree period devoid of obligations. Many factors cause stress and anxiety in teenagers, such as the pressures of school, complicated family dynamics, juggling homework, and extracurricular activities, adjusting to puberty, and maintaining a social life. It's no surprise that the typical teenager nowadays experiences stress levels that are higher than adults.

What Makes Coping With Difficult Emotions Important?

It's critical to have a healthy strategy to deal with difficult emotions, whether you're stressed, anxious, angry, or experiencing any other difficult emotion. Many of us are guilty of resorting to unhealthy coping mechanisms, such as binge-watching Netflix, losing ourselves in video games, indulging in excessive amounts of unhealthy snacks, or even abusing alcohol and drugs.

The issue with these unhealthy coping mechanisms is that they don't address the underlying cause of the problem and are ineffective in helping teens who are experiencing anxiety. Your challenging emotions may simply get worse over time if you don't find a helpful strategy to deal with them. Fortunately, there are several strategies for dealing with those feelings, such as online counseling.

Beginning the process of employing healthy coping mechanisms

So how do you as a teenager start the process of changing your bad behaviors with positive, fruitful ones? The first step is just to become more conscious of any coping skills you now employ that aren't truly benefiting you. Perhaps you reach for your phone and start scrolling through social media as soon as you have the recognizable anxiety twinge. Or perhaps whenever you feel overwhelmed, you reach for the food cabinet. You shouldn't and shouldn't need to feel guilty about using these coping strategies. The fact that you've established these coping mechanisms demonstrates that you've tried to manage your challenging emotions in some way.

It's now time to take your bad behaviors and transform them into helpful coping methods that will enhance both your mental and physical health. You may put your phone down and take a few deep breaths if you catch yourself reaching for it, or you could even step outside and go for a quick stroll. Fresh fruit or nuts, which have many health advantages and can give you some energy to deal with the problem at hand, are an excellent substitute for those sugary snacks.

Examining your emotions and considering where they are originating from is also crucial. You'll probably discover that the same feelings keep bubbling to the surface again and over again if you choose to ignore how you're feeling. However, you'll have much more control over those difficult feelings if you can isolate the source of the problem.

The secret is to commit to them and make them a regular habit if you want to create long-lasting healthy coping strategies. Even though it could be challenging at first, it ought to become second nature with time. You'll need to consciously choose to utilize healthy coping techniques in place of harmful coping methods while you're waiting for that time to come.

Healthy coping techniques for teens

We've put up the list below to give teenagers who wish to manage their emotions in a healthy way a wide range of possibilities, from anxiety coping skills for teens to general teenage coping skills. Check out the following choices after reading the list to see if any of them appeal to you. You might even want to compile your list of coping mechanisms that you can use repeatedly when stress or other unwelcome feelings start to wear you down.

Activities

These coping mechanisms are intended to assist you in calming down and regaining control over your emotions so that you can face the current circumstance with more confidence and strength.

- Write, draw, paint, sculpt, or produce art in another way.

- Perform musically, dance, or sing.

- Take a hot shower or bath.

- Drive or go for a walk.

- Organize and tidy up your environment.

- Read a section of a book called Communication.

One of the best ways to cope with challenging emotions is through social interaction and support.

- Speak to someone you can trust, like your parents, other family members, or friends.

- Send yourself or a friend a note.

- Find a way to assist others by offering your services or volunteering.

- Cozy up to a pet

- Play the scenario you're anxious about in your head

Positive thinking entails more than just adopting an optimistic outlook on life. There are other techniques as well to teach your brain to concentrate on the positive aspects of life. The advice provided below can gradually help you become more resilient in a range of circumstances while also naturally encouraging you to be more observant of yourself and life in general.

- Make a list of your blessings and come up with answers to the problem at hand.

- Make a list of all of your advantages and good qualities.

- If you're having trouble deciding, develop a list of the benefits and drawbacks.

Letting go of tension

You sometimes just need a way to let out strong feelings without hurting yourself or anyone else.

- A funny YouTube video or show should be seen.

- Punch or scream into a pillow

- Exercise will help you move your body.

- Contemplate crying.

Changes in Lifestyle

Your lifestyle has a big impact on how much stress you experience and how well you can deal with it. If you want to feel more empowered and have better mental health, think about making some adjustments in your life.

- Eat nutritious foods to fuel your body.

- Cut back on caffeine

- Make it a habit to breathe deeply every day.

- To stay hydrated, consume lots of water.

Spiritual Techniques
Spiritual coping mechanisms can help you feel accepted and at peace whether or not you practice a religion.

- Meditate and be mindful.

- Pray

- Embrace the outdoors

- Participate in a worthwhile cause by volunteering.

Are you having trouble coping? Don't be afraid to ask for professional assistance if you require it, or even if you don't believe you do but still believe you could benefit from it. You can seek assistance from your school counselor if you're a teen. In some circumstances, it could be vital to talk to your parents so they can look into finding a therapist for you (or themselves). TeenCounseling is an excellent substitute for in-person counseling for teenagers and is also cost-effective.

Chapter Eleven

Problem-Solving Skills

Why problem-solving abilities are crucial

Every day, everyone must find solutions to issues. However, we must acquire the talents necessary to achieve this; they are not something we are born with.It's advantageous to have the following skills when tackling issues:

- Think and listen carefully weigh your options, and respect the needs and perspectives of others.
- Work toward concessions through negotiation.

These are life skills, and both social and professional contexts place a high value on them.Teenagers develop a positive self-image when they discover techniques and methods for resolving issues and handling disagreements independently. They are better equipped to decide well for themselves.

Six steps to problem-solving
Talking and bargaining are frequently effective ways to address issues. If you are having trouble finding a solution, the following 6 actions can help. They can be used to resolve the majority of issues, including interpersonal conflicts and challenging decisions or choices.

Your child will be more likely to apply these techniques when dealing with their issues or interpersonal difficulties if you practice them with them at home.

1. Identify the issue first
Finding the precise nature of the issue is the first stage in problem-solving. This can make the issue more universally understood. It's preferable to bring everyone who is impacted by the issue together before formulating a plan of action.

It's best to tackle challenges with your child when everyone can think clearly and is calm. This will increase your child's motivation to find a solution. Decide on a time when you won't be interrupted, and then thank your child for helping to find the solution.

2. Consider the causes of the issue.

Assist your child or children in identifying the issue's origin and cause. Answers to inquiries like these might be helpful to take into account:

- What makes this matter so much to you?
- What is the purpose of this?
- What do you believe could happen?
- What is bothering you?
- The worst that could occur is what?

Without arguing or debating, try to listen. This is your opportunity to learn more about how your child is doing. Try using the phrases "I need," "I want," "I feel," etc., and encourage your child to do the same. Encourage your child to keep the focus on the problem and to avoid placing blame at this time.

A little healthy conflict is normal, but too much isn't good. Use conflict resolution techniques if you find yourself at odds with your child frequently. This is advantageous for your family relationships and can reduce the likelihood of future conflict.

3. Generate a list of potential remedies for the issue.
Make a list of all the potential solutions that you and your child could use to solve the issue. You're seeking a variety of options, both sensible and less sensible. Be careful not to debate or judge these at this time.

Start them off with some of your ideas if your child struggles to come up with solutions. You could start by offering a crazy idea; unusual or humorous suggestions often lead to more sensible ones. Make an effort to jointly generate at least five potential answers.

Here are some potential solutions, for instance, if your kids are fighting over playing Xbox:

- So that you won't have to share, we buy another Xbox.

- The two of you agree on the times that each of you can use the Xbox.

- You all have designated days to use the Xbox.

- You each get 30 minutes a day to use the Xbox.

- You should put your Xbox away until next year.

4. Consider the issues with the solutions.

Consider each suggested solution's benefits and drawbacks separately. Everyone will then feel as though their suggestions have been taken into account.

The solutions that you all agree are unacceptable should be crossed off the list. For instance, you might all concur that letting your kids decide whether or not to share the Xbox is not an option because they've already tried it and it didn't work.

Cross off the options with more drawbacks than advantages from your list of pros and cons for the remaining solutions. Next, give each answer a score between 0 and 10, with 10 being the best.

Your child should be able to implement and complete the solution you and your child decide on. If none of them seem to be working, return to step 3 and try some other approaches. To get a variety of new ideas, it might be beneficial to speak with others, such as other family members.

You might not always be able to come up with a solution that pleases everyone. You ought to be able to get to an agreement that everyone can live with, though, by bargaining and making concessions.

5. Implement the recommendation

Plan out every detail of the solution once you've reached an agreement on it. Putting these things on paper and including them can be helpful.

- Exactly what will each person do?
- When will they carry it out?
- What is necessary to implement the solution?

In the case of the Xbox, it was decided that "You each get to use the Xbox for 30 minutes a day." The solution's implementation could be planned as follows:

- Exactly what will each person do? At various points throughout the day, your kids will take turns.

- When will they carry it out? After completing their schoolwork, one youngster will have the first turn. When their pals are playing after supper, the other child will get their turn.

- What's necessary? So that each youngster knows when to stop, you need a timer.

You might also discuss a future meeting time to assess how the solution is performing. You may demonstrate to your child that you appreciate their participation in major decisions and that you believe they are capable of handling their difficulties by investing time and effort into helping them develop their problem-solving abilities. This will improve your bond with your child.

6. Examine the results of your problem-solving efforts.

Once your child or children have carried out the plan, you should evaluate how it went and, if necessary, assist them in repeating the procedure.

Keep in mind that not all solutions will be successful and that your child will need to give the solution time to function. They may need to try several different solutions at times. Being able to adjust when things don't go as planned is a necessary component of problem-solving effectively.

The following are inquiries to pose to your child:

- What has been effective?
- What hasn't been that effective?
- What could you or we change to make the solution operate more efficiently?

If the answer doesn't work, start over at step 1 of this problem-solving approach. It's possible that the issue wasn't what you first believed it to be or that the solutions weren't quite right.

Chapter Twelve

Time Management Skills

While your teen may feel fine waiting until the very last minute to finish her math assignment or her high school science lab, procrastination can be a major issue in the future.

She might discover that putting off her work until the last minute leaves her vulnerable to an unanticipated illness, crisis, or another issue that prevents her from finishing it. It's unlikely that her future employer or college professors will accept late work or the justifications that go along with it.

Teenagers who don't develop time management skills run the risk of developing procrastination as a lifelong habit. Furthermore, putting off tasks until the last minute could result in issues like relationship issues and high levels of stress.

Teach your teen responsible behavior from a young age. To do that, she must effectively manage her time so that she doesn't need your help or reminders all the time.

Time management is crucial. It can be very busy in high school. The adult world, however, can be even busier. So it's crucial to start your teen's time management education right away.

The advantages of effective time management include:
- Better capacity for decision-making
- Better performance at work and school Greater independence and responsibility More opportunities to unwind and relax
- Lessening anxiety as school deadlines or test dates approach

Instruction in Time Management

The typical schedule for teenagers is fairly regimented. Their after-school activities and school day are organized for them. Because of this, many of them fail to learn how to effectively use their free time.

You can take the following actions to impart important time management skills to your teenager :

1. Tell your teen to record his schedule in writing.
If your teen isn't careful, social media or video games could easily take up all of his time. Teach him how to plan his day so he can allot time for his responsibilities, including his work and homework. To avoid feeling like he hasn't done anything enjoyable, encourage him to schedule his free time as well.

2. AVOID nags.
It may be tempting to badger your teenager or provide constant reminders. However, nagging your teen to do his homework or chores repeatedly makes him less accountable. 1 Establish guidelines for your expectations and, when necessary, carry out the resulting sanctions.

3.Develop routines with your adolescent. Encourage your teen to develop good habits by having him complete his chores right after school. 2 He won't have to spend time pondering his next move once he gets into the habit of carrying out tasks in a particular order.

4. Provide time-management tools to your teen. Help your teen identify the tools that will work best for him, whether it's a planner in which he writes everything down or an app that organizes his schedule. Discuss the value of making a schedule and using lists to prioritize his time effectively.

5. Facilitate her goal-setting by offering advice.
Talk to your teen about her objectives. Next, assist her in determining how much time per day she needs to dedicate to achieving that goal. Setting goals is a great way to help her manage her time, whether she chooses to apply for scholarships one Saturday afternoon each month

or wants to exercise for 30 minutes three times per week.

6. Please assist your teen in setting priorities.
Teenagers frequently experience scheduling conflicts. A church event, a basketball game, and a birthday celebration might all fall on the same day. Talk to your teen about setting priorities for activities based on his commitments and values.

7. Set an example of effective time management.
Your teen will imitate you if you consistently arrive late or frequently miss deadlines. Show your teen that you are capable of completing the most important tasks in a given day by practicing time management in your own life.

8. Put restrictions on electronics.
If she's not careful, your teen might lose countless hours on social media or playing video games. Establish guidelines that will assist her in developing wholesome digital device and cellphone habits.

9.Supporting your teen in developing time management skills.

There will be times when she underestimates the time needed for a project or forgets a deadline. Remind her that Rome wasn't built in a day and encourage her to learn from her errors.

Chapter Thirteen

Decision-Making Skills

Every day, both major and minor decisions are made. All ages of kids should learn how to make decisions because parents want their kids to become independent, dependable, and content adults.People who can weigh their options and make decisions are frequently more successful in life. Giving young children a small choice between two options can help them develop decision-making skills early on. Teenagers will need to learn to make more decisions as they grow older and become more independent. Teenagers will advance toward this goal by developing and using a decision-making and problem-solving process.

More and more choices that affect teens must be made. From both their triumphs and failures, they will grow and learn. If their parents make the majority of their decisions, they won't be prepared to do so when they are adults.

How can you, as their parent, assist them in developing good decision-making skills? Allow them to make decisions while showing them how to go through the steps in the decision-making process. You could frequently be a part of the process and set a good example by acting in the right way. Additionally, this is an excellent chance for you and your child to start talking.

How to Make Decisions and Solve Problems in Six Steps

1. Find and specify the issue. What would be the best result or objective?

2. List all potential options and alternatives.

Put many ideas on paper using a brainstorming technique. Even if the teen's initial suggestion doesn't seem feasible to you, it's crucial to let them write it down. Ask if you can suggest if they seem to be having trouble getting started (give them some time to reflect first). Making it ridiculous may inspire them to speak freely.

Keep going until you run out of options or ideas. Remind yourself not to pass judgment. It's just a collection of thoughts.

3. Analyze your options.

With your support, advice, and encouragement, let the teen consider his or her options. If you notice a point they are overlooking, ask them if you can make it. By requesting their consent before making a point, you increase the likelihood that they will pay attention to what you have to say and won't take it as a criticism of their opinions or way of thinking.

The following queries can assist the teen in assessing their options: Is it cruel? Is that painful? Is it unjust? Is it untrue? Does it fit the purpose?

4. Choose just one.
The problem's solution mustn't make things worse for someone else.

5. Create a strategy, then follow through on it.
The hardest step is probably this one. If the other person does not approve of their selection, they might have to return to the list of possibilities.

6. Consider the issue and the solution.
Even though it is probably the decision-making process' most overlooked step, learning depends on it. Think about: What caused the issue? Can a future occurrence of a similar issue be avoided? In

what way was the current issue resolved? Alternatively, they can learn from their mistakes and take responsibility for finding a different solution. If their suggestion didn't work, refrain from saying "I told you so."